Looking at Science
How Things Change

Looking at
LIFE CYCLES

HOW DO PLANTS AND ANIMALS CHANGE?

Angela Royston

Enslow Elementary
an imprint of
Enslow Publishers, Inc.
40 Industrial Road
Box 398
Berkeley Heights, NJ 07922
USA

http://www.enslow.com

Enslow Elementary, an imprint of Enslow Publishers, Inc.

Enslow Elementary® is a registered trademark of Enslow Publishers, Inc.

This edition published in 2008 by Enslow Publishers, Inc.

Copyright © 2008 The Brown Reference Group plc

Library of Congress Cataloging-in-Publication Data

Royston, Angela
  Looking at life cycles : how do plants and animals change? / Angela Royston.
     p. cm. — (Looking at science : how things change)
  Summary: "An explanation of life cycles of different plants and animals, as well as people"—Provided by publisher.
  Includes bibliographical references and index.
  ISBN-13: 978-0-7660-3091-6 (alk. paper)
  ISBN-10: 0-7660-3091-1 (alk. paper)
1. Life cycles (Biology)—Juvenile literature. I. Title.
  QH501.R69 2008
  571.8—dc22

                                    2007024513

Printed in the United States of America
042010 Lake Book Manufacturing, Inc., Melrose Park, IL

10 9 8 7 6 5 4 3 2

To Our Readers: We have done our best to make sure all Internet Addresses in this book were active and appropriate when we went to press. However, the author and the publisher have no control over and assume no liability for the material available on those Internet sites or on other Web sites they may link to. Any comments or suggestions can be sent by e-mail to comments@enslow.com or to the address on the back cover.

Every effort has been made to locate all copyright holders of material used in this book. If any errors or omissions have occurred, corrections will be made in future editions of this book.

For The Brown Reference Group plc
Project Editor: Sarah Eason
Designer: Paul Myerscough
Picture Researcher: Maria Joannou
Children's Publisher: Anne O'Daly

Photo and Illustration Credits: The Brown Reference Group plc (illustrations), pp. 7, 9, 19; Dreamstime, pp. 4, 20B, 23T; FLPA/S. & D. & K. Maslowski, p. 11, Mitsuaki Iwago, p. 24B; istockphoto, pp. 1, 4BL, 4BR, 8B, 10, 12, 18, 18B, 20, 21B, 22B, 24, 25T, 28B, 29R; Photos.com, p. 6; Shutterstock, pp. 2, 6B, 8, 13T, 14, 15T, 16, 16B, 22, 26, 26B, 27B, 28, 30; Geoff Ward (illustrations), pp. 17, 21.

Cover Photo: istockphoto

Contents

What is a life cycle?

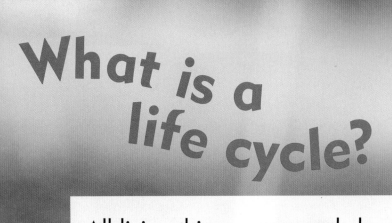

All living things grow and change during their lives. They also reproduce, or have babies. We call these changes a life cycle.

An animal's life cycle begins when it is born or hatches from its shell. The young animal then grows into an adult and has young of its own.

All plants and animals have
a life cycle. Most plants
begin life as a seed.

This gardener is ▼
planting a seed.
It will grow into
a plant.

How does pollen spread?

Some plants have bright flowers. Insects, such as bees, land on the flowers and pick up pollen on their legs. They carry it to the flowers on other plants. The wind can also spread pollen.

Pollen is made in a flower's anthers.

Pollen from another flower of the same kind enters the stigma.

The pollen fertilizes egg cells in the flower's ovary.

Did you know that a flower has tiny egg cells? They can be fertilized by pollen from another plant of the same kind. A fertilized egg cell becomes a seed.

What is the life cycle of a plant?

A plant begins to grow when a seed falls into damp soil. Roots grow down into the soil. A shoot grows upward. The shoot grows leaves. Flowers grow and blossom.

shoot
seed

roots

▼ The seeds from one flower may grow into many new plants.

Pollen fertilizes egg cells within the flowers, forming seeds. Fruit or nuts may grow around the seeds. When the seeds fall to the ground, the life cycle begins again.

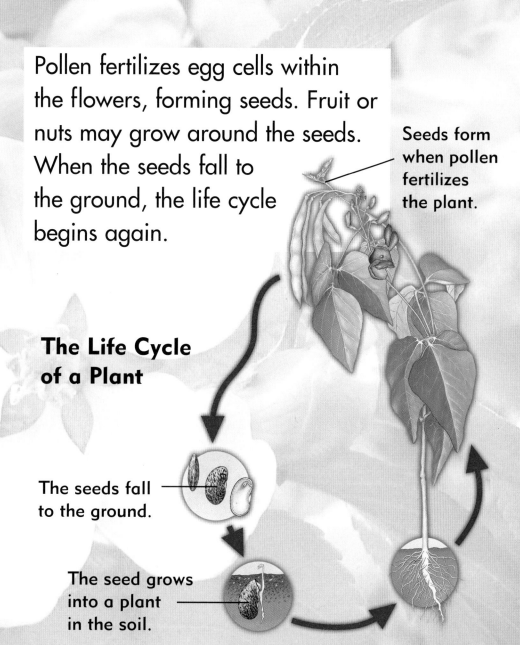

Seeds form when pollen fertilizes the plant.

The Life Cycle of a Plant

The seeds fall to the ground.

The seed grows into a plant in the soil.

9

Why do birds lay eggs?

Every bird begins life as an egg. The mother bird lays the egg in a nest. The bird sits on the eggs to keep them warm. A chick grows inside each egg.

A duck is a bird. These ▶ eggs have been laid by a mallard duck.

A chick grows inside its egg for about 21 to 33 days. When the chick is ready to hatch, it pecks a hole in the egg shell. Slowly, it breaks the shell apart and crawls out.

This duckling is ▼ hatching from its egg.

Why do ducklings swim in a line?

Young ducklings swim in a line behind their mother so they do not get lost. As they grow older, they swim farther away from the mother duck.

▼ Ducklings follow their mother wherever she goes.

When they are about two months old, ducklings are able to take care of themselves.

As ducklings grow bigger, their fluffy feathers fall out. Stronger feathers grow in their place.

How do ducks find a mate?

In spring, adult birds look for a mate. Many male birds have nice feathers. They show them off to attract a female bird.

▲ These male (left) and female (right) mallard ducks are mates. Mallard ducks keep the same mate for life.

▲ Mallard ducks build their nest near a pond or river. They make it from grass and other plants.

The male bird fertilizes the female's eggs. When she lays them, they will grow into ducklings. A new life cycle has begun.

Why do fish lay so many eggs?

A female fish lays hundreds of eggs. A male fish fertilizes them. Many of the eggs are eaten by other fish or animals.

The Life Cycle of a Fish

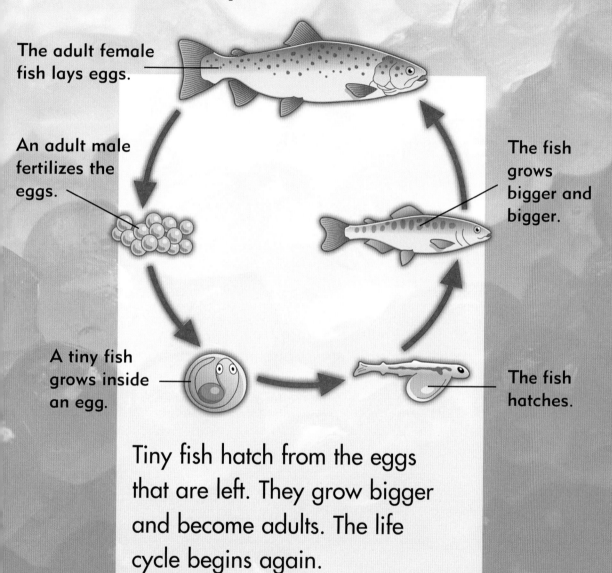

The adult female fish lays eggs.

An adult male fertilizes the eggs.

A tiny fish grows inside an egg.

The fish grows bigger and bigger.

The fish hatches.

Tiny fish hatch from the eggs that are left. They grow bigger and become adults. The life cycle begins again.

How do tadpoles turn into frogs?

A frog begins life as a tadpole in an egg. When it hatches, the tadpole lives in water. It breathes through gills, like a fish. As it gets bigger, it swims to the surface to breathe in air through its lungs.

▼ As it changes into a frog, the tadpole grows back legs.

back legs

The tadpole grows front and back legs. It loses its tail and changes into a frog. It leaves the pond and lives mainly on the land. When it is fully grown, the frog finds a mate and they reproduce.

The Life Cycle of a Frog

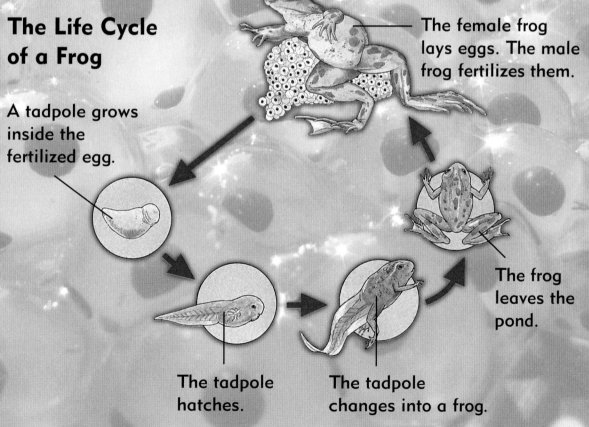

The female frog lays eggs. The male frog fertilizes them.

A tadpole grows inside the fertilized egg.

The frog leaves the pond.

The tadpole hatches.

The tadpole changes into a frog.

How do caterpillars grow?

A caterpillar starts life as an egg. The egg is laid on a leaf. When it hatches, the caterpillar begins to eat the leaf.

When the caterpillar is fully grown, it spins a cocoon around itself. It slowly changes into a butterfly inside the cocoon.

A caterpillar grows inside an egg.

The butterfly breaks out of the cocoon. It finds a mate and lays eggs.

The caterpillar hatches from its egg.

The caterpillar spins a cocoon and changes into a butterfly.

The Life Cycle of a Butterfly

After a few weeks, it breaks out of the cocoon and flies away. It finds a mate and lays eggs of its own. The life cycle begins again.

How do mammals feed their young?

Mammals are animals that feed their babies with milk from their bodies. Most mammals have hair or fur. Dogs, cats, cows, bears, and people are all mammals.

When they are ▶ very young, mammals feed on their mother's milk.

▲ Young dogs learn by play fighting and hunting with their mother.

The mother looks after her babies until they are strong enough to care for themselves. When they are fully grown, adult mammals look for a mate. Then they have babies of their own.

Why do kangaroos have pouches?

As soon as a baby kangaroo is born, it climbs inside its mother's pouch. The pouch protects the baby as it grows bigger. Baby kangaroos feed on their mother's milk inside the pouch.

◀ A baby kangaroo is called a joey. It is very tiny when it is born.

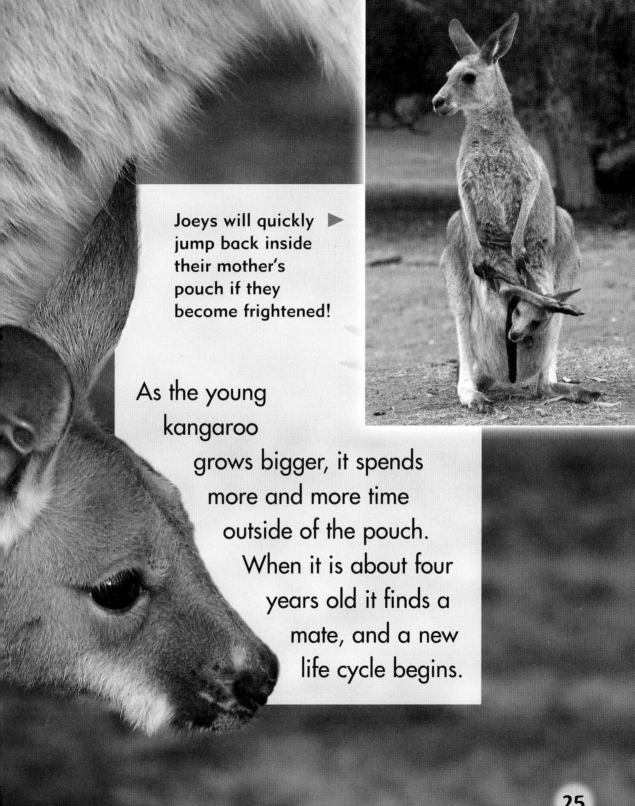

Joeys will quickly ▶
jump back inside
their mother's
pouch if they
become frightened!

As the young
kangaroo
grows bigger, it spends
more and more time
outside of the pouch.
When it is about four
years old it finds a
mate, and a new
life cycle begins.

Do humans have a life cycle, too?

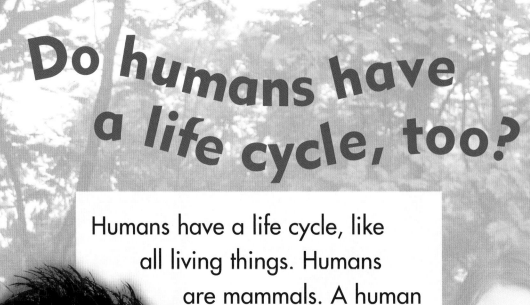

Humans have a life cycle, like all living things. Humans are mammals. A human baby feeds on its mother's milk. The baby grows into a child who can walk and talk.

▼ **Human babies feed from their mother's breasts or from a bottle.**

Parents give their children love and protection. They feed them and give them somewhere safe to live.

Humans look after their young for longer than any other animal. They may have children of their own when they become adults, and the life cycle starts again.

What do I know about life cycles?

1. Ask an adult to help you with this activity:
   - Plant some sunflower seeds in a pot of damp soil.
   - Put the pot in a warm, sunny place. Water it every day.
   - When the seeds begin to grow and get bigger, you may need to move them into separate pots.

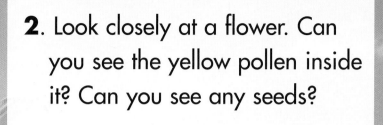

2. Look closely at a flower. Can you see the yellow pollen inside it? Can you see any seeds?

3. In spring, look for birds flying to and from their nests. Are they carrying grass to build a nest, or food for their chicks?

4. In summer, look for caterpillars and butterflies. How are they different from each other?

Words to Know

adult — Fully grown animal.

anthers — Part of a flower that makes pollen.

cocoon — A covering some insects make around their body.

fertilize — When an egg or egg cell is changed so that it can grow into a young plant or animal.

gills — Openings in an animal's body through which it breathes underwater.

hatch — To break out of an egg shell.

life cycle — A process in which plants and animals grow and change from birth through adulthood, when they can reproduce.

ovary — Part of a plant or animal that contains its egg cells.

pollen — Tiny particles from a flower that fertilize the egg cells of another flower to form seeds.

reproduce — To make another young animal or plant.

stigma — Part of a flower that receives pollen from another flower.

tadpole — Baby frog that has not yet shed its tail.

Learn More

Books

Greenaway, Theresa. *Plant Life*. New York: Hodder Wayland (2006).

Kalman, Bobby. *Animal Life Cycles: Growing and Changing*. New York: Crabtree Publishing Company (2006).

Ross, Michael. *Life Cycles*. Brookfield, Conn.: Millbrook Press (2003).

Web Sites

Backyard Plants
www.backyardnature.net/botany.htm

Butterfly and Moth Life Cycle
http://bsi.montana.edu/web/kidsbutterfly/life-cycle

Index